F
Disciples

Radical Disciples

A course for new Christians preparing for baptism

Revised Edition

Paul Beasley-Murray

Baptist Union
of Great Britain
www.baptist.org.uk

2005

Published on behalf of The Baptist Union of Great Britain
by Nigel Lynn Publishing & Marketing Ltd
106 High Street, Milton under Wychwood, Chipping Norton
Oxfordshire, OX7 6ET, United Kingdom

The Baptist Union of Great Britain
Baptist House, 129 Broadway, Didcot
Oxfordshire, OX11 8RT, United Kingdom

First published 1996
Second edition published 2005

British Library Cataloguing in Publication Data
Data available

ISBN   0 901472 34 4

1 3 5 7 9 10 8 6 4 2

Cover design by Wheeler & Porter Ltd, Banbury
Printed in the United Kingdom
on acid-free paper by
The Alden Group, Oxford

CONTENTS

THE AUTHOR

Paul Beasley-Murray grew up in a Christian home and so has always been aware of the love of God in Christ. He still vividly remembers the Sunday evening when at the age of eight he 'opened the door' of his heart to the Lord Jesus and welcomed him in to his life (see Revelation 3.20). Five years later he was baptised in 'Salemskapelle', the main Baptist church in Zurich, Switzerland, and has been in membership of Baptist churches ever since.

After studying at the universities of Cambridge, Manchester and Zurich, he served for two years with the Baptist Missionary Society in Kisangani, where he taught New Testament and Greek at the National University of Congo (Zaire). On his return from Africa he pastored the Baptist church in Altrincham, Cheshire for thirteen years, before becoming Principal of Spurgeon's College, London, from 1986 to 1992.

He is currently the senior minister of Central Baptist Church, Victoria Road South, Chelmsford, Essex.

A prolific author, he has written a number of books and booklets for Baptist Union Publications, which together now form the 'radical' series of publications.

Radical Believers: the Baptist way of being the church

Radical Disciples: a course for new Christians preparing for baptism

Radical Leaders: a guide for elders and deacons

Happy Ever After? A 'radical' workbook for couples preparing for marriage

Other 'radical' publications are planned!

Preface to the Second Edition

Apart from minor amendments, the major difference between the first and second edition is that the Scripture quotations have been taken from *Today's New International Version of the Holy Bible* (TNIV) published in 2005 (copyright International Bible Society, British edition published by Hodder & Stoughton), as distinct from the older *New International Version of the Holy Bible* (NIV), first published in 1973. The TNIV builds on the NIV with about 7% of changes: these changes include the introduction of 'generic language where the meaning of the text was intended to include both men and women'; other changes relate to 'clarity' and 'sentence structure and grammar'.

If we are to be effective Christians we need to programme our minds, just as a computer is only effective as its 'memory' is programmed. Hence at the end of each section, a memory verse is suggested.

If you wish to do more, there is much to be said for learning off by heart the order of the books of the Bible. Start with the New Testament, go on to Genesis–Psalms, and finish with Proverbs–Malachi. The benefit is that you will be able to find your way through the Bible so much more easily.

INTRODUCTION

A call to discipleship

Just before he ascended to his Father, the risen Lord Jesus gave what the Duke of Wellington once called 'the marching orders of the church'. Here in the Great Commission is to be found the basis of this course for new Christians.

> All authority in heaven and on earth has been given to me. Therefore go and make disciples of all nations, baptising them in the name of the Father and of the Son and of the Holy Spirit, and teaching them to obey everything I have commanded you. And surely I am with you always, to the very end of the age. (Matthew 28.18–20)

As Christians we are called to be 'disciples', i.e. we are called to be followers of the Lord Jesus, committing ourselves to him not only in baptism but also in the ongoing task of going Christ's way. In the New Testament the term 'Christian' is only found three times, whereas the term 'disciple' is used 269 times. 'Christian' is just a label, whereas the word 'disciple' contains a sense of movement and direction. As disciples of the Lord Jesus we never 'graduate' from his school—we are always learning from him, we are always dependent on him. Baptism does not mark the end of the process of becoming a Christian—it simply marks the end of the beginning!

A call to radical discipleship

Radical disciples are those who root their lives in Jesus and in God's Word, the Bible. The word 'radical' comes from the Latin word *radix*, which means 'root'. In this baptismal course we will see how the Baptist understanding of Christian discipleship is rooted in Scripture. The aim of the course is to encourage people to think about ten different aspects of discipleship by examining in depth a limited number of Scripture passages all grouped together under one common theme. Furthermore, recognising that many people today cannot easily find their way through the Bible, every Scripture passage to which reference is made is reproduced in full—in *Today's New International Version* of the Bible.

A word to the course leader

You will notice that the comments introducing each passage of Scripture are limited. In one sense this creates more work for the course leader, for inevitably these comments need expansion. Yet the limited nature of these comments actually makes it easier to use this course with people of very different backgrounds and of quite different ages. A useful reference book for the course leader is *Radical Believers: the Baptist Way Of Being The Church* (Baptist Union of Great Britain 2002, second edition 2005) by Paul Beasley-Murray.

RESPONDING TO CHRIST

Christian basics

Here we have one of the earliest Christian creeds—possibly learnt by Paul when he too was preparing for baptism. The death and resurrection of Jesus are at the heart of the Christian faith. Notice how the death of Jesus is 'for our sins'.

1 Corinthians 15.3–5

For what I received I passed on to you as of first importance: that Christ died for our sins according to the Scriptures, that he was buried, that he was raised on the third day according to the Scriptures, and that he appeared to Cephas, and then to the Twelve.

Repenting

Repentance is the first step in becoming a Christian. Repentance always involves a change of direction—it is not just a feeling sorry, but an actual turning away from sin, and instead going the way of Jesus …

Acts 2.37–38

When the people heard this, they were cut to the heart and said to Peter and the other apostles, 'Brothers, what shall we do?' Peter replied, 'Repent and be baptised, every one of you, in the name of Jesus Christ for the forgiveness of your sins. And you will receive the gift of the Holy Spirit.'

Believing

The second step in becoming a Christian is believing in God's love for us. It is almost incredible that God should love us all so much that he should give his Son. It is also almost incredible that God's offer of life is open to all who believe, whoever we are, whatever we may have done.

John 3.16

For God so loved the world that he gave his one and only Son, that whoever believes in him shall not perish but have eternal life.

Receiving

As we in faith give ourselves to God, God in his turn gives himself to us. He gives himself to us in sending his Spirit. It is the Holy Spirit who makes God real in our lives and satisfies our spiritual hunger. We were made to relate with God—now we have become what we were intended to be.

Romans 8.9–16

If anyone does not have the Spirit of Christ, they do not belong to Christ ... And if the Spirit of him who raised Jesus from the dead is living in you, he who raised Christ from the dead will also give life to your mortal bodies because of his Spirit, who lives in you ... The Spirit you received brought about your adoption to sonship. And by him we cry, 'Abba, Father.' The Spirit himself testifies with our spirit that we are God's children.

Following

Jesus never pretended the Christian life was easy. There is a cost—no life of our own! For when Jesus calls us to 'take up our cross' he calls us to go the way of death. Following Jesus involves more than easy 'believism'—it involves a commitment of a lifetime.

Mark 8.34–36

Then he called the crowd to him along with his disciples and said: 'Whoever wants to be my disciple must deny themselves and take up their cross and follow me. For whoever wants to save their life will lose it, but whoever loses their life for me and for the gospel will save it. What good is it for you to gain the whole world, yet forfeit your soul?'

Memory verse   John 3.16

OBEYING CHRIST

The command of Christ

Baptism is no optional extra. Jesus expects his disciples to commit themselves to him in the waters of baptism. Baptism is part of the normal Christian life. If we love Jesus, we will want to obey him (John 15.14).

Matthew 28.18–20

Jesus said, 'All authority in heaven and on earth has been given to me. Therefore go and make disciples of all nations, baptising them in the name of the Father and of the Son and of the Holy Spirit, and teaching them to obey everything I have commanded you. And surely I am with you always, to the very end of the age.'

The example of Christ

Although there are differences between the baptism of Jesus and ours, nonetheless like Jesus we must be prepared to submit ourselves to the will of God and 'do what God requires' (GNB). Like Jesus, we must be obedient.

Matthew 3.13–17

Jesus came from Galilee to the Jordan to be baptised by John. But John tried to deter him, saying, 'I need to be baptised by you, and do you come to me?' Jesus replied, 'Let it be so now; it is proper for us to do this to fulfil all righteousness.' Then John consented. As soon as Jesus was baptised, he went up out of the water. At that moment heaven was opened, and he saw the Spirit of God descending like a dove and alighting on him. And a voice from heaven said, 'This is my Son, whom I love; with him I am well pleased.'

The practice of the early church

In New Testament times there was no such person as an unbaptised Christian. Baptism was part of the process of becoming a Christian. Baptism was integral to conversion.

Acts 8.12

When they believed Philip as he proclaimed the good news of the Kingdom of God and the name of Jesus Christ, they were baptised, both men and women.

A declaration of union with Christ

Baptism is a dramatic way of declaring our solidarity with Jesus, crucified and risen. In this 'watery grave' we identify ourselves with Jesus, who died and rose for us, and resolve to die to self and to live for him.

Romans 6.3–4

Don't you know that all of us who were baptised into Christ Jesus were baptised into his death? We were therefore buried with him through baptism into death in order that, just as Christ was raised from the dead through the glory of the Father, we too may live a new life.

A sign of cleansing

In baptism we acknowledge that we are sinners who stand in need of Christ's cleansing power. In this 'bath' our sins are washed away as we commit ourselves to the Christ who died for us.

Acts 22.16

[Ananias said to Paul] 'Now what are you waiting for? Get up, be baptised and wash your sins away, calling on his name.'

A confession of faith

Baptism is the moment when we proclaim our allegiance to Jesus and publicly declare in front of others that we belong to Jesus and to his people. It is never a private occasion. So we need to ensure that we bring along a good number of friends when we are baptised.

1 Timothy 6.12

Fight the good fight of the faith. Take hold of the eternal life to which you were called when you made your good confession in the presence of many witnesses.

A rite of initiation

Baptism is the normal way of entering the church. We are baptised 'to form one body' (literally 'into the body' of Christ). Therefore church membership is an integral part of baptism. To commit ourselves to Jesus involves committing ourselves to the people of Jesus.

1 Corinthians 12.13

For we were all baptised by one Spirit so as to form one body—whether Jews or Gentiles, slave or free—and we were all given the one Spirit to drink.

A sign of the Spirit's presence

The Spirit is God's gift to all who put their trust in Jesus. Not surprisingly baptism, where we express our trust in Jesus, is often associated with the gift of God's Spirit. See also Matthew 3.13–17, Acts 2.38 and 1 Corinthians 12.13.

Ephesians 1.13–14

And you also were included in Christ when you heard the word of truth, the gospel of your salvation. When you believed, you were marked in him with a seal, the promised Holy Spirit, who is a deposit guaranteeing our inheritance until the redemption of those who are God's possession—to the praise of his glory.

Memory verses   Matthew 28.18–20

GROWING IN CHRIST

Growing up in the family

We cannot live the Christian life on our own; we need the company of other Christians. For we will only grow into maturity as we receive both encouragement and discipline from within the family of Christ.

Ephesians 4.14–16

Then we will no longer be infants, tossed back and forth by the waves, and blown here and there by every wind of teaching and by the cunning and craftiness of people in their deceitful scheming. Instead, speaking the truth in love, we will in all things grow up into him who is the Head, that is, Christ. From him the whole body, joined and held together by every supporting ligament, grows and builds itself up in love, as each part does its work.

Feeding on God's Word

We need too to develop a system of daily Bible reading. We need to feed our minds as also our spirits on God's Word. Only so will we grow.

1 Peter 2.2

Like newborn babies, crave pure spiritual milk, so that by it you may grow up in your salvation.

Learning from God's Word

The Bible is to be trusted—for God has wonderfully 'inspired' men and women to tell the story of his saving acts. The teaching found within the Bible is also to be obeyed—for here is God's pattern for our life together.

2 Timothy 3.15–17

The Holy Scriptures … are able to make you wise for salvation through faith in Christ Jesus. All Scripture is God-breathed and is useful for teaching, rebuking, correcting and training in righteousness, so that all God's people may be thoroughly equipped for every good work.

Learning to pray

As we begin to grow, we learn to speak—and listen—to God in prayer. Our Heavenly Father delights in his children bringing to him their concerns.

Matthew 7.7, 9–11

'Ask and it will be given to you; seek and you will find; knock and the door will be opened to you … Which of you, if your son asks for bread, will give him a stone? Or if he asks for a fish, will give him a snake? If you, then, though you are evil, know how to give good gifts to your children, how much more will your Father in heaven give good gifts to those who ask him!'

Submitting to the Father's will

As we grow we discover that sometimes God says 'no' to our prayers. Sometimes this is for our own good—sometimes it is for the good of others. Although at the time we may not understand why our prayers are not answered in the way we wish, we can always trust God that his ways are best.

Luke 22.42

'Father, if you are willing, take this cup from me; yet not my will, but yours be done.'

Living in Christ

It is in our ongoing developing relationship with Jesus that we find the strength for daily living. Our own resources are limited. Much as we wish to be active in Christ's service, our activism must be balanced by times of quiet 'resting' in Jesus.

John 15.4–5

'Remain in me, as I also remain in you. No branch can bear fruit by itself; it must remain in the vine. Neither can you bear fruit unless you remain in me. I am the vine; you are the branches. If you remain in me and I in you, you will bear much fruit; apart from me you can do nothing.'

Making time for God

If Jesus found it necessary to make time—and space! —for God, then surely it must be even more true of us. All of us need to find time within the busyness of our lives to focus on God and discover his direction and strength for our lives.

Mark 1.35

Very early in the morning, while it was still dark, Jesus got up, left the house and went off to a solitary place, where he prayed.

Memory verses   John 15.4–5

FOLLOWING CHRIST

Getting our priorities straight

A mark of Christian discipleship is that God comes first in our lives. Jesus promises that God will look after the needs of those who are concerned above everything else to do what he requires.

Matthew 6.33

'Seek first his (God's) kingdom and his righteousness, and all these things will be given to you as well.'

Producing fruit

Another mark of Christian discipleship is that we reflect the Lord Jesus in the kind of people we are. This comes about as we allow his Spirit to have control of our lives

Galatians 5.22–25

The fruit of the Spirit is love, joy, peace, patience, kindness, goodness, faithfulness, gentleness and self-control ... Those who belong to Christ Jesus have crucified the sinful nature with its passions and desires. Since we live by the Spirit, let us keep in step with the Spirit.

Forgiving our enemies

To reflect the Lord Jesus in our lives means that we will forgive those who have hurt us. Forgiveness does not mean minimising the wrong done; it means letting go of our feelings of anger and bitterness.

Matthew 6.14–15

'If you forgive others when they sin against you, your heavenly Father will also forgive you. But if you do not forgive others their sins, your Father will not forgive your sins.'

Going against the stream

It's not easy following Christ. Whether it be in our relationships with the opposite sex or in the way in which we conduct ourselves at work, our values are different. It takes courage to go the way of Jesus.

Romans 12.2

Do not conform to the pattern of this world, but be transformed by the renewing of your mind. Then you will be able to test and approve what God's will is—his good, pleasing and perfect will.

Discovering God's will

The Spirit guides us in various ways—through Scripture, through circumstances, through reasoning, through the advice of Christians friends, as also through inner promptings.

Acts 16.9–10

During the night Paul had a vision of a man of Macedonia standing and begging him, 'Come over to Macedonia and help us.' After Paul had seen the vision, we got ready at once to leave for Macedonia, concluding that God had called us to preach the gospel to them.

Dealing with temptation

There can be no room for complacency—temptation is inevitable when we are seeking to follow the Lord Jesus. Giving in to temptation, however, need not be inevitable!

1 Corinthians 10.12–13

If you think you are standing firm, be careful that you don't fall! No temptation has overtaken you except what is common to us all. And God is faithful; he will not let you be tempted beyond what you can bear. But when you are tempted, he will also provide a way out so that you can endure it.

Dealing with failure

There are times when we fail Christ—and fail one another. But, however badly we may have failed, in Jesus there is always a new beginning. When we have fallen in the race of faith, he allows us to pick up ourselves and continue from where we fell.

1 John 1.7–9

The blood of Jesus, his Son, purifies us from all sin … If we confess our sins, he is faithful and just and will forgive us our sins and purify us from all unrighteousness.

Memory verse   Matthew 6.33

WORSHIPPING CHRIST

Giving God the glory

Worship is the occasion when we acknowledge God's 'worth'. Christian worship in particular centres on the new thing that God has done in Jesus. Sunday by Sunday we come to celebrate the resurrection of the Crucified.

Psalm 96.1–3

Sing to the Lord a new song; sing to the Lord, all the earth. Sing to the Lord, praise his name; proclaim his salvation day after day. Declare his glory among the nations, his marvellous deeds among all peoples.

Listening to God speak

Through the reading and preaching of the Bible, God speaks to his people. Like the Roman soldier Cornelius, God's people are blessed when they come together expecting to receive a word from God.

Acts 10.33

'Now we are all here in the presence of God to listen to everything the Lord has commanded you to tell us.'

Responding in song

Inevitably as we hear God speak, we want to respond in praise. Down through the ages God's people have used a variety of worship styles to sing their praises.

Colossians 3.16

Let the message of Christ dwell among you richly as you teach and admonish one another with all wisdom, through psalms, hymns and songs from the Spirit; singing to God with gratitude in your hearts.

Bringing our prayers

An important part of worship is the intercessions, when in prayer we bring before God the needs both of the church and of the world. Intercession is an expression of our love for others. Not to pray is not to love.

1 Timothy 2.1–2

I urge, then, first of all, that petitions, prayers, intercession and thanksgiving be made for everyone—for kings and all those in authority, that we may live peaceful and quiet lives in all godliness and holiness.

Remembering the Lord Jesus

Christian worship climaxes in the celebration of the Lord's Supper. Here we remember not only that Jesus died for us, but also that he rose again and is with us now. We also look forward to the day when Jesus shall return again in glory and shall establish his Kingdom for ever and ever.

I Corinthians 11.23–26

For I received from the Lord what I also passed on to you: the Lord Jesus, on the night he was betrayed, took bread, and when he had given thanks, he broke it and said, 'This is my body, which is for you; do this in remembrance of me.' In the same way, after supper he took the cup, saying, 'This cup is the new covenant in my blood; do this, whenever you drink it, in remembrance of me.' For whenever you eat this bread and drink this cup, you proclaim the Lord's death until he comes.

Expressing our fellowship with one another

The Lord's Supper is by definition a communal act. As we come to the Communion Table, we come together. It is here that we sense our unity with one another—here we pray for one another. It is vital that we are right with one another.

I Corinthians 11.27–29

So then, whoever eats the bread or drinks the cup of the Lord in an unworthy manner will be guilty of sinning against the body and blood of the Lord. Everyone ought to examine themselves before they eat of the bread and drink of the cup. For those who eat and drink without discerning the body of Christ eat and drink judgment on themselves.

Renewing our vows

Whenever the Lord's Supper is meaningful, it will end in renewed dedication to the service of God. This is the moment when we may renew our baptismal vows of love and loyalty to our Lord.

Psalm 116.12–14

What shall I return to the Lord for all his goodness to me? I will lift up the cup of salvation and call on the name of the Lord. I will fulfil my vows to the Lord in the presence of all his people.

Memory verses   Psalm 116.12–14

LIVING TOGETHER IN CHRIST

Belonging to one another

When we are born again, we are born into a family. We belong to one another. And because we belong to one another, we have a responsibility for one another. Church membership in the first place is about commitment to one another.

1 Corinthians 12.25–27

(All the parts of the body) should have equal concern for each other. If one part suffers, every part suffers with it; if one part is honoured, every part rejoices with it. Now you are the body of Christ, and each one of you is a part of it.

Loving one another

Love is more than a feeling. Love if it is to be real must be expressed. Jesus washed his disciples' feet, and then went on to give his life for them on a Cross. Jesus calls us to be equally down-to-earth in our loving. Others must see the difference, if they are to believe.

John 13.34–35

'A new command I give you: love one another. As I have loved you, so you must love one another. By this everyone will know that you are my disciples, if you love one another.'

Greeting one another

Greeting one another involves more than saying hello. It involves more than showing physical affection. It involves knowing the name of the other— knowing the situation of the other. Love must always have a cutting edge.

Romans 16.15–16

Greet Philologus, Julia, Nereus and his sister, and Olympas and all the Lord's people who are with them. Greet one another with a holy kiss.

Encouraging one another

We all have our ups and downs. We all need encouragement. Encouragement is actually vital for personal growth and development. Children, for instance, who are encouraged at home and at school often do well in life. The same is true in the Christian family. Don't forget that encouragement can also be expressed in actions as well as in words!

1 Thessalonians 5.11

Encourage one another and build each other up.

Bearing one another's burdens

In cases where Christians badly fail their Lord and discipline is necessary, restoration should always be in view. There is no place for judgmentalism. Rather we are to draw alongside and bring help. What is true of the 'burden' of failure, is also to be true of other 'burdens' in life. God does not intend us to grin and bear it alone

Galatians 6.1–2

Brothers and sisters, if someone is caught in a sin, you who live by the Spirit should restore that person gently. But watch yourselves, or you also may be tempted. Carry each other's burdens, and in this way you will fulfil the law of Christ.

Praying for one another

All of us need prayer, because all of us in one way or another need God's healing touch in our lives. We may not necessarily be physically sick, but instead we may be spiritually 'below par'. If, however, we are to be blessed by the prayers of others, then we must be open about our needs.

James 5.16

Confess your sins to each other and pray for each other so that you may be healed.

Covenanting together

Sometimes church membership is described as entering into a 'covenant' with one another. A covenant may be likened to a binding agreement. When we welcome others into church membership we are formally committing ourselves to love one another and stand by one another whatever the cost.

1 Samuel 18.3; 23.15–16

Jonathan made a covenant with David because he loved him as himself … While David was at Horesh in the Desert of Ziph, he learned that Saul had come out to take his life. And Saul's son Jonathan went to David at Horesh and helped him to find strength in God.

Memory verses   John 13.34–35

LIVING TOGETHER UNDER THE LORDSHIP OF CHRIST

Jesus is Lord of his church

Some churches are governed by bishops, others through elders or through church councils. For Baptists it is the church meeting which is the ultimate authority in their life together. Yet when Baptists come together in church meeting they are concerned to engage not in a form of democracy (government by the people for the people) but rather in a form of theocracy (God ruling through the church meeting). Jesus is to be lord of his church.

Colossians 1.18

And he is the head of the body, the church ... so that in everything he might have the supremacy.

Appointing leaders

When the first 'deacons' were appointed, it was left to the church—and not to the apostles—to choose seven men. The church meeting continues to be the place where leaders are appointed.

Acts 6.3, 5–6

'Brothers and sisters, choose seven men from among you who are known to be full of the Spirit and wisdom' ... This proposal pleased the whole group. They chose Stephen, a man full of faith and of the Holy Spirit; also Philip, Procorus, Nicanor, Timon, Parmenas, and Nicolas from Antioch, a convert to Judaism. They presented them to the apostles, who prayed and laid their hands on them.

Administering finance

When a particular financial need was made known to the church, the disciples—and not the elders alone—were involved in the decision-making process. The church meeting continues to be the place were budgets are approved.

Acts 11.29–30

The disciples, as each one was able, decided to provide help for the believers living in Judea. This they did, sending their gift to the elders by Barnabas and Saul.

Admitting members

At an early period in its life the early church was faced with the question of admitting members from a non-Jewish background. Although the apostles and the elders took the initiative in thrashing the matter through, the church as a whole was involved in making the decision to welcome Gentile believers into their midst. The church meeting continues to be the place where membership matters are decided.

Acts 15.22

Then the apostles and elders, with the whole church, decided …

Exercising discipline

Jesus makes clear that the ultimate recourse in discipline is not to the church leaders, but to the church itself. When all else fails, the church meeting has the final authority.

Matthew 18.15–17

'If a brother or sister sins, go and point out the fault, just between the two of you. If they listen to you, you have won them over. But if they will not listen, take one or two others along, so that "every matter may be established by the testimony of two or three witnesses." If they still refuse to listen, tell it to the church; and if they refuse to listen even to the church, treat them as you would a pagan or a tax collector.'

Honouring leaders

The New Testament concept of the church meeting does not rule out the need for leaders. Leadership is part of the God-given task of those who preach and teach.

1 Timothy 5.17

The elders who direct the affairs of the church well are worthy of double honour, especially those whose work is preaching and teaching.

Submitting to leaders

The church delegates some of its authority to leaders, authority which the leaders are free to use until the church withdraws its recognition of them. Good leadership has always the well-being of the church in view.

Hebrews 13.17

Have confidence in your leaders and submit to their authority, because they keep watch over you as those who must give an account. Do this so that their work will be a joy, not a burden, for that would be of no benefit to you.

Memory verse   Colossians 1.18

SERVING CHRIST

Discovering our gifts

Everybody is gifted! What is more we all vary in the gifts we have been given. Our task is to discover our gifts and then, by God's grace, to develop them in his service.

Romans 12.6–8

We have different gifts, according to the grace given to each of us. If your gift is prophesying, then prophesy in accordance with your faith; if it is serving, then serve; if it is teaching, then teach; if it is to encourage, then give encouragement; if it is giving, then give generously; if it is to lead, do it diligently; if it is to show mercy, do it cheerfully.

Using our gifts for the good of others

God does not give gifts to make us feel good about ourselves—but rather to enable us to serve others. Precisely how we serve will vary from situation to situation.

1 Corinthians 12.7–11

Now to each one the manifestation of the Spirit is given for the common good. To one there is given through the Spirit a message of wisdom, to another a message of knowledge by means of the same Spirit, to another faith by the same Spirit, to another gifts of healing by that one Spirit, to another miraculous powers, to another prophecy, to another distinguishing between spirits, to another speaking in different kinds of tongues, and to still another the interpretation of tongues. All these are the work of one and the same Spirit, and he distributes them to each one, just as he determines.

Serving beyond the church

A key role for those gifted with leadership roles in the church is to equip God's people to serve in the world. In other words, it is not so much a question of the members supporting the leaders in their particular sphere of service, but rather of the leaders supporting the members in the work to which God has called and gifted them!

Ephesians 4.11–12

Christ ... gave the apostles, the prophets, the evangelists, the pastors and teachers, to equip God's people for works of service.

Serving in the wider community

In the ancient world salt not only gave flavour, it also acted as a preservative. In other words Jesus expects his disciples to exercise an antiseptic influence and be a positive influence for good.

Matthew 5.13

'You are the salt of the earth.'

Serving through good time management

Time is a precious gift from God. All of us are to be good managers of our time. There are various ways of wasting time. We can waste time, for instance, by failing to distinguish the important from the urgent.

Ephesians 5.15–16

Be very careful, then, how you live—not as unwise but as wise, making the most of every opportunity …

Serving through giving

Money too is a gift from God. Therefore we need to think carefully on how we manage our financial resources—and then give generously.

2 Corinthians 9.6–8

Remember this: whoever sows sparingly will also reap sparingly, and whoever sows generously will also reap generously. Each of you should give what you have decided in your heart to give, not reluctantly or under compulsion, for God loves a cheerful giver. And God is able to bless you abundantly, so that in all things at all times, having all that you need, you will abound in every good work.

Serving through proportionate giving

In the Christian church there are no membership dues. Rather we are called to give a realistic proportion of our income. A tenth is often a good guide— but remember, God sees not just what we give, but also what we keep for ourselves. For some Christians a double-tithe might even be appropriate!

1 Corinthians 16.2

On the first day of every week, each one of you should set aside a sum of money in keeping with your income.

Memory verse   Matthew 5.13

WITNESSING TO CHRIST

Witnessing where we are

Witnessing to Jesus begins right where we are—the place where we live, work, study and play. It is in our 'Jerusalems' where we can often be the most effective.

Acts 1.8

Jesus said: 'You will receive power when the Holy Spirit comes on you; and you will be my witnesses in Jerusalem, and in all Judea and Samaria, and to the ends of the earth.'

Telling our story

Witnessing involves telling others about what Jesus has done for us—and what he means for us now. Not everybody may have a dramatic story to share, but everybody may be able to tell speak of the difference Jesus makes to life! There's a lot to be said for writing down our story and sharing it with a friend to ensure that it is jargon-free and to-the-point.

John 9.25

'One thing I do know. I was blind but now I see!'

Being at the ready

Witnessing normally involves responding to opportunities which are given to us. Brashness does the Christian cause no favours. There is a time to be silent, but also a time not to be silent.

1 Peter 3.15

Always be prepared to give an answer to everyone who asks you to give the reason for the hope that you have. But do this with gentleness and respect.

Making friends for Jesus

Effective witnessing involves making friends with people outside the church. Unfortunately the older we grow in our Christian faith, the more we are tempted to live our lives in a Christian ghetto. Jesus deliberately rubbed shoulders with non-religious people—and so should we.

Matthew 11.19

The Son of Man came eating and drinking, and they say, 'Here is a glutton and a drunkard, a friend of tax collectors and sinners.'

Inviting people home

Effective witnessing usually entails inviting people into our homes before we invite them to our church. It is within the context of the home that people will hopefully sense our normality—and also our faith! Friendship evangelism takes time, but can also be very fruitful.

Luke 5.27–29

Jesus … saw a tax collector by the name of Levi sitting at his tax booth. 'Follow me', Jesus said to him, and Levi got up, left everything and followed him. Then Levi held a great banquet for Jesus at his house, and a large crowd of tax collectors and others were eating with them.

Networking for Jesus

Bridges of friendship are often built as we make the most of our network of relationships. Most of us link into at least four distinct areas of relationships:

+ the family (e.g. parents, spouse, children, brothers and sisters)
+ work (e.g. the boss, our colleagues) or school (fellow students and teachers)
+ leisure (e.g. football team, sports club)
+ general social contacts (e.g. neighbours)

Here are people to befriend—and bring to Jesus. It's helpful to make a list of all those who fall into these categories—and then pray that God will give us an opportunity to share the good news of Jesus with them.

Mark 5.19

Jesus said, 'Go home to your own people and tell them how much the Lord has done for you, and how he has had mercy on you.'

Going out on a limb for Jesus

Witnessing takes many and varied forms. What may be right for one person, may be wrong for another. We need to be imaginative, but also sensitive, to each and other situation.

1 Corinthians 9.22

To the weak I became weak, to win the weak. I have become all things to all people so that by all possible means I might save some.

Memory verse   1 Peter 3.15

Expressing Christ's Love to Others

Bringing in the kingdom

The kingdom of God is not so much an area, but God in action. Jesus not only proclaimed the coming of the kingdom of God, he also demonstrated the kingdom in action as he transformed people's lives. Indeed, the very 'signs' of the kingdom confirmed the truth of his claims. So also today, kingdom action must accompany kingdom preaching if the gospel is to be good news to the poor. Here is the basis not only for social service but also for political action.

Matthew 11.2–5

John (the Baptist) ... sent his disciples to ask him, 'Are you the one who was to come, or should we expect someone else?' Jesus replied, 'Go back and report to John what you hear and see: the blind receive sight, the lame walk, those who have leprosy are cleansed, the deaf hear, the dead are raised, and the good news is proclaimed to the poor.'

Caring for the needy

At the end of time when Christ sits in judgement on the nations of the world, he will welcome into his kingdom those who have shown practical love to those in need. Note too that no one is too insignificant to be the object of our care.

Matthew 25.35–36, 40

'I was hungry and you gave me something to eat, I was thirsty and you gave me something to drink, I was a stranger and you invited me in, I needed clothes and you clothed me, I was ill and you looked after me, I was in prison and you came to visit me ... Truly I tell you, whatever you did for one of the least of these brothers and sisters of mine, you did for me.'

Loving the stranger

Love for our neighbour means that we cannot pass by on the other side in the face of need. It also means that we can never restrict love to people like ourselves. Love knows no ethnic, cultural or religious boundaries.

Luke 10.33–34, 36–37

'But a Samaritan, as he travelled, came where the man was; and when he saw him, he took pity on him. He went to him and bandaged his wounds, pouring on oil and wine. Then he put the man on his own donkey, brought him to an inn and took care of him ... Which of these three do you think was a neighbour to the man who fell into the hands of robbers?' The expert in the law replied, 'The one who had mercy on him.' Jesus told him, 'Go and do likewise.'

Helping the poor

Where there is no social conscience, there God's love is not present. Just as there was no limit to the concern of Jesus for our need, so too there should be no limit to our concern for those with less than ourselves.

I John 3.16–17

This is how we know what love is: Jesus Christ laid down his life for us. And we ought to lay down our lives for one another. If any one of you has material possessions and sees his brother or sister in need but has no pity on them, how can the love of God be in you?

Acting the peacemaker

Peacemaking is more than smoothing over ruffled feathers; rather it is concerned to establish relationships that are right because they are rooted in righteousness. Peacemaking is not about compromises—it is about dealing with the root causes of those things which divide us.

Matthew 5.9

'Blessed are the peacemakers, for they will be called children of God.'

Going the Jesus' way

Jesus not only preached good news—he was good news. He fed the hungry and healed the sick. The love of God was 'made flesh'. To go the way of Jesus is to be involved in 'holistic mission', caring for bodies as well as souls.

John 20.21

Jesus said, 'Peace be with you! As the Father has sent me, I am sending you.'

Memory verse   John 20.21

BELONGING TO THE WIDER FAMILY OF CHRIST

Christians ...

When we are baptised we are joining the world-wide family of God. In Jesus, all barriers of race and gender, social standing and church background, are overcome. True, distinctions still remain—but they no longer count.

Galatians 3.26–28

In Christ Jesus you are all children of God through faith, for all of you who were baptised into Christ have clothed yourselves with Christ. There is neither Jew nor Gentile, slave nor free, male nor female, for you are all one in Christ Jesus.

... and Baptist Christians

When we become a church member, we join that part of the family of God called 'Baptist'. It's the largest Protestant family in the world—with almost 40 million baptised members. Baptists believe that their way of being the church is not just one of several options open to them—rather their study of God's Word leads them to believe that this is God's way for living their life together. The Baptist way of being the church includes:

Confessing the faith

Baptists practise *believers'* baptism. At the end of the day the emphasis is not on the quantity of water, but rather on the quality of faith. Baptism expresses the believer's response of faith to the grace of God.

Acts 22.16

'And now what are you waiting for? Get up, be baptised and wash your sins away, calling on his name.'

Living together in community

Along with believers' baptism is the Baptist emphasis on the church as a body of committed believers. For Baptists the church is a local community of believers, gathered together out of the world, who have committed themselves to Christ and to one another.

Acts 2.41–42

Those who accepted his message were baptised, and about three thousand were added to their number that day. They devoted themselves to the apostles' teaching and to fellowship, to the breaking of bread and to prayer.

Living under the lordship of Christ

The local church is where the heart of Baptist life is. Baptists adopt a congregational system of church government, believing that God rules through church meetings made up of members of a local church. Each Baptist church therefore is self-governing.

Acts 13.1–3

In the church at Antioch there were prophets and teachers: Barnabas, Simeon called Niger, Lucius of Cyrene, Manaen (who had been brought up with Herod the tetrarch) and Saul. While they were worshipping the Lord and fasting, the Holy Spirit said, 'Set apart for me Barnabas and Saul for the work to which I have called them.' So after they had fasted and prayed, they placed their hands on them and sent them off.

Associating with others

In spite of their emphasis on the local church, Baptists believe not in independency but inter-dependency. Just as no individual Christian can afford to be a loner, neither can any local church go it alone.

Ephesians 4.4–6

There is one body and one Spirit, just as you were called to one hope when you were called; one Lord, one faith, one baptism; one God and Father of all, who is over all and through all and in all.

Serving one another

From their beginnings, Baptists have treasured the Reformation principle of 'the priesthood of all believers'. Baptists believe that all God's people have equal access to God and in turn have equal responsibility to serve God.

1 Peter 2.9

But you are a chosen people, a royal priesthood, a holy nation, God's special possession, that you may declare the praises of him who called you out of darkness into his wonderful light.

Sharing the Faith

Baptists have been characterised by a passion for the gospel. Indeed, their rite of believers' baptism emphasises the necessity of conversion.

2 Corinthians 5.20

We are therefore Christ's ambassadors, as though God were making his appeal through us. We implore you on Christ's behalf: be reconciled to God.

Memory verses   Ephesians 4.4–6

A BAPTISMAL CHECK-LIST

Practicalities to be sorted out before the day of baptism

Have you invited your friends, relatives and neighbours to the service? Remember, they might be more inclined to come if you put on a lunch party after the service! If there is going to be a good number of visitors, let the church know so that space at the front of the church can be reserved for them.

In most churches, the candidate gives a short testimony before the baptism. Have you written out your testimony? A page is provided at the back of this book that you may wish to use. Make sure that it does not simply tell the story of your journey to faith, but that it also tells of what Jesus means to you today. It is often helpful to include a Bible verse that has a special meaning to you.

Have you invited a friend (normally of the same sex) to sit next to you during the service and to hold your towel (and glasses) while you are being baptised?

You will need to have a complete change of clothes. Remember, ladies, that white clothes can become transparent when wet! Most people tend to wear a T-shirt and trousers, but make sure it is a plain T-shirt (no advertising please!).

In many churches, candidates are encouraged to choose a song or a verse of a hymn, which the congregation sings as the baptism takes place. If this is the custom of your church, have you chosen your song or hymn? Remember, the words need to be appropriate, and the tune needs to be known by most people.

On the day of the baptism itself

Arrive in plenty of time. The ministers and deacons of your church may well want to pray with you before the service.

There is no need to feel nervous today. You will be borne up by the prayers of the church.

When you give your testimony, ready slowly and clearly. Don't worry, however, if you stumble. Everybody is 'on your side'.

Your minister or the person baptising you will probably ask a question along the lines of: 'Do you profess repentance toward God and faith in Jesus as

Saviour and Lord?' To this you need to say a loud 'I do.' The minister will then say: 'We therefore baptise you in the name of the Father, the Son and the Holy Spirit. Amen.'

Don't worry about the mechanics of baptism. Instead, as you are baptised, focus your thoughts on Jesus. Say to him: 'Jesus, I love you. You gave your life for me, and I now give my life to you.'

Expect God to bless you with a fresh out-pouring of his Spirit. For when we commit ourselves to God, God in turn commits himself to us.

MY TESTIMONY